TIDE POOL

TIDE POOL

PHOTOGRAPHED BY
FRANK GREENAWAY

WRITTEN BY
CHRISTIANE GUNZI

DK PUBLISHING, INC.

DK

A DK PUBLISHING BOOK
www.dk.com

Senior editor Christiane Gunzi **Senior art editor** Val Wright
Editor Deborah Murrell **Art editor** Julie Staniland
Design assistant Lucy Bennett
Production Louise Barratt
Illustrations Nick Hall
Index Jane Parker
Managing editor Sophie Mitchell
Managing art editor Miranda Kennedy
U.S. editor B. Alison Weir

Consultants
Geoff Boxshall, Theresa Greenaway, Paul Hillyard, Gordon Howes, Charles Hussey, Gordon Patterson, Kathie Way

With thanks to Neil Welton of Dorking Aquatic Centre, who supplied some of the animals in this book.
Endpapers photographed by Breck P. Kent, Oxford Scientific Films, Ltd.

First American Edition, 1992
First Paperback Edition, 1998
2 4 6 8 10 9 7 5 3

First published in the United States by
DK Publishing, Inc., 95 Madison Avenue, New York, New York 10016.
Copyright © 1992 Dorling Kindersley Limited, London

Library of Congress Cataloging-in-Publication Data
Greenaway, Frank.
Tide Pool/photographed by Frank Greenaway; written by Christiane Gunzi. – 1st American ed.
p. cm. – (Look closer)
Includes index
Summary: Discusses the different kinds of plants and animals that can be found in tide pools
and how they interact with each other.
ISBN 0-7894-2972-1
1. Marine biology–Juvenile literature. 2. Tide pools–Juvenile literature.
[1. Marine animals. 2. Tide pool ecology. 3. Ecology.]
I. Gunzi, Christiane. II. Title. III. Series.
QH91.16.G74 1992
574.92–dc20
92-52823–CIP–AC

Color reproduction by Colourscan, Singapore
Printed and bound in Singapore by Imago

CONTENTS

Life in a tide pool 8

False flowers 10

Hunting dogs 12

Crusty crab 14

Cross crab 16

Shore swimmers 18

Water weeds 20

Sea spines 22

Big mouth 24

Rock stars 26

Little lemon 28

Index and glossary 29

Look for us, and we will show you the size of every animal and plant that you read about in this book.

LIFE IN A TIDE POOL

ON ROCKY SHORES, CLOSE to the sea, there are tide pools filled with seawater. They range from small, shallow puddles high up on the shore to huge, deep holes nearer to the sea. All of them are home to dozens of different animals and plants. Tide pools form as the sea washes over the shore twice a day. These tides bring fresh oxygen and food to the wildlife. Some animals spend their whole life in one pool, while others swim in and out with the tides. Between tides, some of the smaller pools become too warm, and begin to dry up. Many of the animals take shelter under cool, damp rocks and moist seaweeds so that their bodies do not dry out before the tide comes in again.

The spiny starfish *(Marthasterias glacialis)* is 5 in. wide and lives in European and North American waters.

The five-bearded rockling *(Ciliata mustela)* is 6 in. long and lives in Northwest European waters.

The shanny *(Lipophrys pholis)* is 4 in. long and lives in European waters.

The short-spined sea scorpion (*Myoxocephalus scorpius*) is 4 in. long and lives in European and North American waters.

The edible crab's *(Cancer pagurus)* shell is 4 in. wide and it lives in European waters.

These sea urchins *(Lytechnicus* species) are 21/2 in. wide and live in European and North and South American waters.

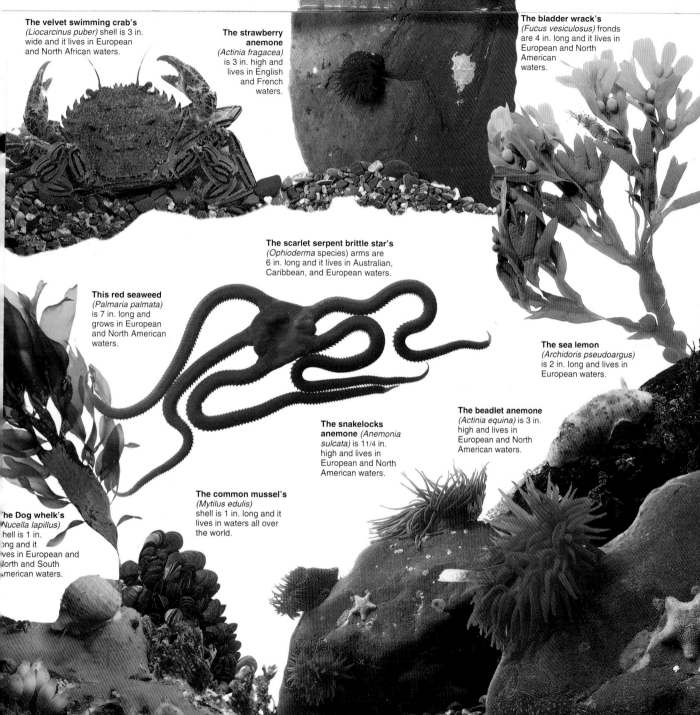

The velvet swimming crab's *(Liocarcinus puber)* shell is 3 in. wide and it lives in European and North African waters.

The strawberry anemone *(Actinia fragacea)* is 3 in. high and lives in English and French waters.

The bladder wrack's *(Fucus vesiculosus)* fronds are 4 in. long and it lives in European and North American waters.

The scarlet serpent brittle star's *(Ophioderma* species) arms are 6 in. long and it lives in Australian, Caribbean, and European waters.

This red seaweed *(Palmaria palmata)* is 7 in. long and grows in European and North American waters.

The sea lemon *(Archidoris pseudoargus)* is 2 in. long and lives in European waters.

The snakelocks anemone *(Anemonia sulcata)* is 11/4 in. high and lives in European and North American waters.

The beadlet anemone *(Actinia equina)* is 3 in. high and lives in European and North American waters.

The common mussel's *(Mytilus edulis)* shell is 1 in. long and it lives in waters all over the world.

he Dog whelk's *Nucella lapillus)* hell is 1 in. ong and it ves in European and lorth and South merican waters.

FALSE FLOWERS

SEA ANEMONES MAY look like harmless flowers, but they are carnivorous (meat-eating) animals. Anemones are related to jellyfish and, like them, most have stinging tentacles to paralyze victims. The sea anemone waits for prey (such as a fish) to swim by, then stings it with its tentacles, and pushes it into its mouth opening. Sea anemones spend most of their lives in one place, attached to rocks or buried in mud. Sometimes they divide themselves in two to make a second anemone. They can also make dozens of tiny copies of themselves, which swim out through the mouth opening. Other kinds of anemones produce minute, slipper-shaped larvae, and these swim away to begin their lives elsewhere.

GUESS WHAT?

The scientific name for sea anemones is *Cnidaria,* which comes from an ancient Greek word meaning "nettle." This is a good name because the tentacles of most kinds of sea anemone can sting, just like the leaves of a nettle.

FAT STRAWBERRY

A strawberry anemone is similar in color and shape to a plump, ripe strawberry. Each time it eats a meal, its body becomes very fat and round. Its tentacles almost disappear inside the body, and they stay there until the anemone needs to eat again.

The tentacles are tucked inside the mouth opening while this strawberry anemone digests its meal.

Sea anemones have soft, jelly-like bodies, with no skeleton.

A suckerlike disk under the column holds on to the rock so tightly that the waves cannot knock the anemone off.

The tentacles wave gently in the current.

This part of the body is called the column.

STINGING SNAKES

Snakelocks anemones hardly ever draw their tentacles back into their bodies. They wave around most of the time, waiting for prey such as small shrimp to brush against them. Fully grown snakelocks anemones have about 200 tentacles, which can measure up to six inches long. Their sting is too mild to hurt a human, and just feels sticky to our touch.

BEADS AND BLOBS

When the tide goes out, beadlet anemones look like small blobs of jelly clinging to the rocks. These anemones are so-named because there is a ring of 24 blue or mauve beadlets, containing extra-strong stinging cells, around the base of the tentacles. The anemone's tentacles do not sting other anemones, but if it is attacked by one of its own kind, the beadlets swell up so that it can use them to defend itself.

During low tide, this beadlet anemone tucks its tentacles inside its body. This prevents it from losing too much precious water.

Close up, you can just see the row of poisonous, mauve beads underneath the tentacles.

Dozens of tentacles surround the mouth to help push prey into the opening.

These pink tips may warn enemies that the tentacles are poisonous.

Each tentacle of this snakelocks anemone is armed with stinging cells.

This beadlet anemone is slowly digesting a small fish that it has caught.

HUNTING DOGS

DOG WHELKS ARE carnivorous (meat-eating) hunters. They creep slowly over the rocks, feeding on mussels, barnacles, and limpets. Whelks are a type of snail and they belong to the group of animals called mollusks. They build shells to protect their soft bodies, using chalk from the water. In spring and autumn, dog whelks gather together to mate. The females lay oval-shaped capsules in cracks in the rock, and each capsule contains hundreds of eggs. After four months, tiny whelks hatch out. They shelter from the waves in crevices until they are almost a half-inch long. Then they leave the safety of the rocks and begin to hunt for themselves.

SOFT CENTERS

Like whelks, mussels are mollusks, with soft bodies inside hard shells. But mussel shells have two halves, called valves, which can open and close when the mussel feeds. Mollusks with shells like this are called bivalves.

This pale-colored dog whelk has been eating the tiny barnacles covering the rock.

This bright orange layer on the rock is a simple animal called a sponge.

UNUSUAL CUTLERY

To feed, the dog whelk pushes a hollow tube called a proboscis between the two valves of a mussel. Then it scrapes out the flesh inside with its filelike tongue, called a radula. The radula can also bore holes through shells, with the help of a special chemical that the dog whelk produces to soften them. Drilling the hole can take as long as three days.

Each capsule contains about 1,000 eggs.

EGG EATERS

During the breeding season, a female dog whelk lays about 10 egg capsules. Each capsule may take up to an hour to lay, and measures about a half-inch long. Only 20 to 30 of the eggs inside each capsule are fertile (able to develop). They survive by eating the other eggs. When this happens, the capsules begin to turn purple.

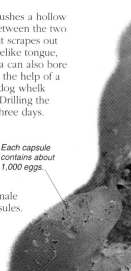

This dog whelk has just found its next meal of mussels.

GUESS WHAT?
Dog whelks can release a purple dye from their bodies. In ancient times, people sometimes used the dye to stain clothing.

PICK A COLOR
Dog whelks can be all sorts of colors, including yellow, pink, orange, and purple. You can tell what a dog whelk feeds on by the color of its shell. Pale-colored dog whelks have eaten barnacles, and dark-colored whelks have fed on mussels. Some whelks, such as this one, have banded shells. Scientists think this may be due to a varied diet.

As a dog whelk grows bigger, it builds up the open end of its shell.

Inside this tube is the proboscis, which the dog whelk uses to feed and breathe.

The tip of the shell is called the apex.

The dog whelk moves around on its large, muscular foot.

This hard disk, called the operculum, functions as a door that seals the dog whelk into its shell, safe from sea birds and crabs.

CRUSTY CRAB

PIECRUST CRABS are well named, because the top part of their shell, called the carapace, looks just like the pastry lid of a pie. These crabs spend much of their time hiding under rocks or seaweed, and they are much less aggressive than their relatives, the velvet crabs. Piecrust crabs eat shellfish, such as shrimp and mussels. They are also great scavengers, eating the remains of dead creatures that they find in the tide pool. Adult piecrust crabs can grow to measure more than six inches across the shell. The little crabs that you see in tide pools are still very young. As they grow, they move down the shore into deeper water. A piecrust crab can live for eight years or more, but the female does not lay eggs until she is about five years old. She may lay more than three million eggs during her lifetime, but only a few will survive to grow into adults.

GUESS WHAT?
These crabs are also called edible crabs. People eat millions of them each year.

RAISING THE ROOF
The crab's body is well protected by its hard outer shell, called the exoskeleton. Like shrimp, lobsters, and other crustaceans, the crab molts (sheds) its exoskeleton every few weeks as it grows, revealing a new one underneath. To get out of the old shell, the crab swallows so much water that the top part of the shell is forced away from the bottom part. The crab then pulls itself out backward.

The fluted edge of the carapace makes this crab look like a piecrust, so it is easy to recognize.

The hard exoskeleton is colored and patterned to blend in well with the pebbles on the beach.

Huge, blunt pincers with serrated (notched) edges grasp food.

Joints on each leg allow the crab to move easily and scuttle away quickly to hide from enemies.

The crab's sharp claws provide it with extra grip for scrambling over rocks.

These sensory hairs are called setae.

HAIRY LEGS
The crab's legs are hairy. These hairs, called setae, are very sensitive. They help the crab feel its way around as it climbs over seaweed, and into dark cracks and crevices in the rock.

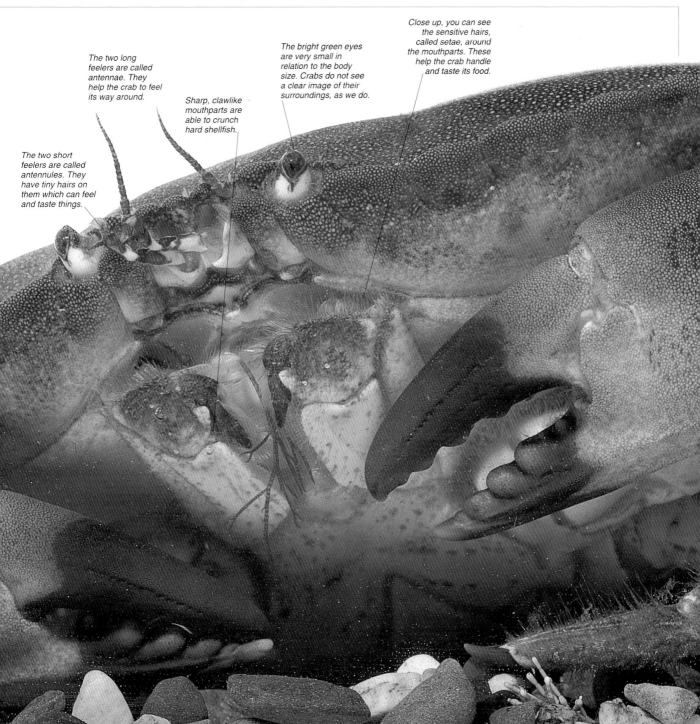

The two long feelers are called antennae. They help the crab to feel its way around.

Sharp, clawlike mouthparts are able to crunch hard shellfish.

The bright green eyes are very small in relation to the body size. Crabs do not see a clear image of their surroundings, as we do.

Close up, you can see the sensitive hairs, called setae, around the mouthparts. These help the crab handle and taste its food.

The two short feelers are called antennules. They have tiny hairs on them which can feel and taste things.

CROSS CRAB

THE COLORFUL VELVET CRAB is one of the most ferocious of all crabs. Its bright red eyes and sharp blue pincers make it look very fierce indeed. Velvet crabs are aggressive predators (hunters), and eat almost anything that they can find in tide pools and on the shore. If a velvet crab is threatened, it rears up on its back legs and holds its sharp pincers out. This makes it look bigger and should frighten its enemy away. If the crab loses a claw in battle, a new one usually grows to replace it. This new claw can be even bigger than the original one. Like all crabs, velvet crabs reproduce by laying eggs. These develop into larvae, and about five weeks later they turn into tiny crabs. An adult female lays millions of eggs during her lifetime, although most of her young will be eaten by fish long before they can grow into crabs.

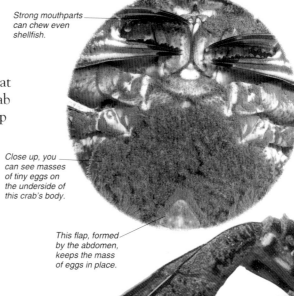

Strong mouthparts can chew even shellfish.

Close up, you can see masses of tiny eggs on the underside of this crab's body.

This flap, formed by the abdomen, keeps the mass of eggs in place.

POWERFUL PADDLER

Velvet crabs are strong swimmers. Their unusual paddle-shaped back legs help them swim away extra fast to escape from predators, such as gulls. These special legs also give velvet crabs their other name of "swimming crabs."

VELVET COAT

The velvet crab is so-named because the top part of its shell, called the carapace, is covered with fine, velvety hairs. Silt (fine pieces of sand) becomes trapped in these hairs, giving the crab its muddy gray color. This coloring is a good disguise when the crab is resting on the sandy bottom of a tide pool.

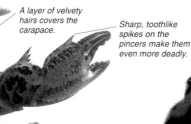

The last joint of the back leg is flattened, so it looks like a paddle.

A layer of velvety hairs covers the carapace.

Sharp, toothlike spikes on the pincers make them even more deadly.

OODLES OF EGGS

This female crab is carrying thousands of eggs under her body. The abdomen (rear part of the body) forms a special flap which holds the eggs in place. After about three months, they hatch into tiny larvae, called zoea. These swim in the open sea among the plankton for several weeks before they begin to change into crabs.

Each pincer is pointed, with serrated (notched) edges for crushing and cutting up food.

Antennae (feelers) on the head help the crab find its way around, even in the dark.

Short feelers called antennules taste things.

GUESS WHAT?
One female velvet crab may produce more than 180,000 eggs at a time.

These beady red eyes scare away predators and warn them not to attack.

This row of sharp spikes helps protect the crab from enemies. The spikes are so sharp that it is difficult to pick the crab up.

Silt is trapped between all these fine hairs.

If one of the legs breaks off, a new one will soon grow to replace it.

Joints allow the legs to bend.

SHORE SWIMMERS

SHANNIES AND ROCKLINGS spend almost all of their lives in tide pools, where they feed on shrimp, prawns, and small crabs. These fish are agile swimmers, and can dart away quickly to a safe corner of the tide pool if they are disturbed. Their coloring helps them blend in well with the seaweed, and keeps them safe from birds and other predators. In the spring and summer, shannies lay eggs in the tide pool, under rocks or in crevices. The male guards the eggs for about eight weeks until they hatch. Shannies only leave the shore during the winter, when they move into deeper water to avoid being thrown against the rocks by rough tides. Rocklings leave their tide pools in early spring to lay their eggs out at sea. The eggs float in the water and gradually develop into larvae, then young fish, which swim ashore to find their own tide pool homes.

FISH FOR DINNER
Young rocklings swim together in huge groups, called schools. These schools of tiny fish provide larger fish, such as mackerel, with a tasty meal. Young rocklings are sometimes nicknamed mackerel midge. Those that survive to grow into adults swim ashore to tide pools in the summer.

SMOOTH SHANNY
Shannies do not have scales covering their bodies, so they are very smooth and slippery. This, together with their long, streamlined body shape, enables them to slip easily between rocks and under seaweed, to find food or hide from enemies.

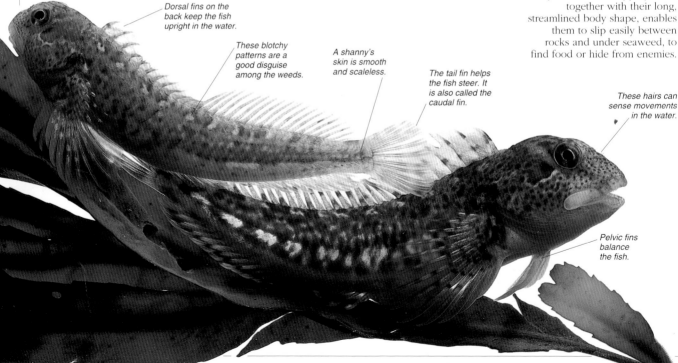

Dorsal fins on the back keep the fish upright in the water.

These blotchy patterns are a good disguise among the weeds.

A shanny's skin is smooth and scaleless.

The tail fin helps the fish steer. It is also called the caudal fin.

These hairs can sense movements in the water.

Pelvic fins balance the fish.

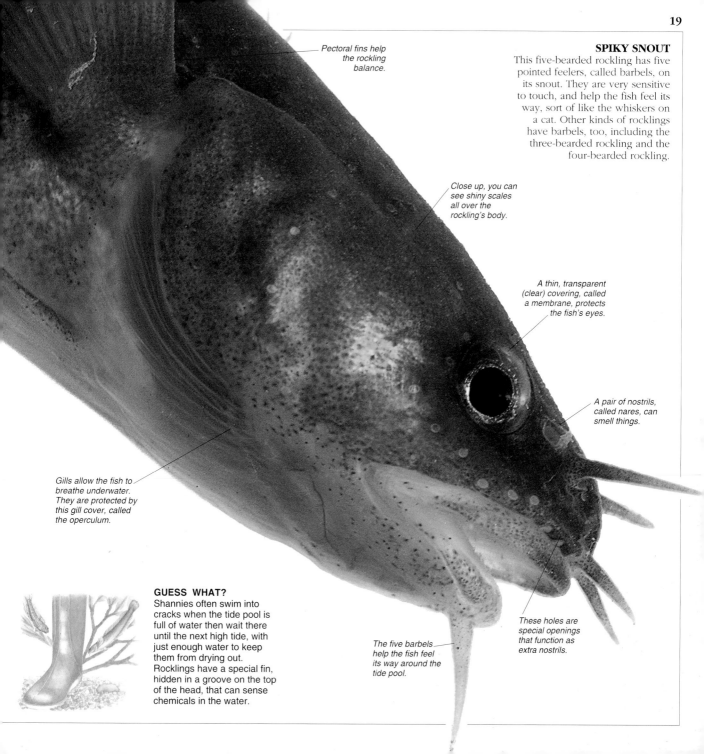

Pectoral fins help
the rockling
balance.

SPIKY SNOUT
This five-bearded rockling has five
pointed feelers, called barbels, on
its snout. They are very sensitive
to touch, and help the fish feel its
way, sort of like the whiskers on
a cat. Other kinds of rocklings
have barbels, too, including the
three-bearded rockling and the
four-bearded rockling.

Close up, you can
see shiny scales
all over the
rockling's body.

A thin, transparent
(clear) covering, called
a membrane, protects
the fish's eyes.

A pair of nostrils,
called nares, can
smell things.

Gills allow the fish to
breathe underwater.
They are protected by
this gill cover, called
the operculum.

GUESS WHAT?
Shannies often swim into
cracks when the tide pool is
full of water then wait there
until the next high tide, with
just enough water to keep
them from drying out.
Rocklings have a special fin,
hidden in a groove on the top
of the head, that can sense
chemicals in the water.

The five barbels
help the fish feel
its way around the
tide pool.

These holes are
special openings
that function as
extra nostrils.

WATER WEEDS

SEAWEEDS BELONG to a group of plants called algae. They have no flowers, no leaves, and no roots. There are many different kinds of seaweeds, including kelps and bladder wracks. They are divided into three groups – green, brown, and red. Green seaweeds often grow in tide pools high up on the shore, brown seaweeds grow in pools farther down the shore, and red seaweeds grow in the shallow waters around the coast. During a storm, all three kinds are washed up onto the shore and flung into tide pools, where they provide food and shelter for many creatures. Seaweeds reproduce by releasing special male cells that pair up with female cells. These produce spores instead of seeds, and they settle on a rock to grow into a new plant. Many of the young seaweed plants are eaten by mussels, limpets, and other mollusks.

GUESS WHAT?
Some kinds of seaweeds grow very long indeed and may measure up to 110 yards in length. Giant kelp grows faster than any other plant – up to 12 inches in one day.

ALGAE ENERGY
Like all plants, seaweeds need light in order to grow. They use the sunlight, together with carbon dioxide and sea water, to make their food in a process called photosynthesis. During photosynthesis, seaweeds give off oxygen, which all animals need to survive.

HOLD ON TIGHT
Instead of roots, seaweeds have a holdfast, so-named because it holds on to a rock. It produces a sticky substance called alginic acid, which acts like glue to help it hold on. The holdfast grips the rock so tightly that sometimes strong waves can break off the stipe (stalk), leaving just a stump and the holdfast behind.

Seaweeds contain a green pigment (coloring) called chlorophyll, which they need for photosynthesis.

This bladder wrack may grow to be more than one yard long.

The stipe is very tough and rubbery. Only the roughest waves can break it.

The holdfast supports the stalklike stipe.

These knobby parts contain the male and female reproductive cells.

FLOATING FRONDS

The round bubbles on this bladder wrack seaweed are called air bladders. They work much like inflatable water wings, making the leaflike fronds float up to the surface of the tide pool toward the sunlight. There they can photosynthesize more easily.

BED AND BREAKFAST

Seaweeds provide shrimp, crabs, fish, and many other creatures with places to hide from predators. In summer, seaweeds also help block out bright sunlight, which can make the water too hot for the animals that live there. Many kinds of animals feed on seaweeds, including sea slugs and snails.

Air bladders filled with gas keep the leafy fronds floating near the surface of the water.

Seaweeds produce a slimy mucus that stops them from getting too dry when the tide goes out.

The red pigment in this seaweed helps it photosynthesize in deep water, where little sunlight gets through.

This bladder wrack belongs to the group of brown seaweeds.

The mass of fronds makes a good hiding place for a shrimp.

All plants contain chlorophyll, but this brown seaweed contains other color pigments as well.

SEA SPINES

THESE UNUSUAL CREATURES look more like prickly tennis balls than living animals, but they are closely related to starfish. Sea urchins and starfish belong to the group of animals called *Echinodermata*, which means "spiny-skinned." Like starfish, sea urchins move around using their special tube feet. They can climb up steep rocks, and cling on tightly when waves splash over them. Despite being covered in sharp spines, sea urchins are sometimes attacked by predators, such as fish. To disguise themselves, they use their tube feet to pick up bits of seaweed and attach them to their spines. Sea urchins release their eggs into the water in the spring. The fertilized eggs develop into tiny larvae. These float around among the plankton and eventually settle down on the sea floor or in a tide pool to grow into adults.

GUESS WHAT?
Sea urchins can live for up to ten years, and during this time, they may produce millions of bright orange, pale yellow, or cream-colored eggs.

GREEDY GRAZER
Sea urchins are omnivores (plant and meat eaters). They graze on tiny plants and animals in the tide pool using the mouth on the underside of the body. The mouth has five powerful, toothlike plates for scraping food off rocks. Inside, it is shaped like an old-fashioned lantern. Sea urchins are sometimes called "Aristotle's lanterns," after the ancient Greek who first wrote about them.

Sea urchins can be all sorts of colors. They often match their surroundings, as this one does.

A TOUGH TEST
A sea urchin's outer skeleton is also called a test. It is made up of plates, which grow larger as the animal grows. These plates touch one another and make the test very strong. Its surface is covered with rows of sharp spines. They wave around as the water flows over them, so they do not snap off easily.

The mouth is at the base of the body, so the sea urchin can feed as it moves along.

The spines are made of chalk. Each one can move without the others.

PERFECT ARMOR

Sea urchins are well-protected by their long spines. These are in rows, and between them are the tube feet. Some of the spines have pincerlike ends. If the sea urchin is attacked by a predator, these special pincers break off and stick in the attacker's skin, where they inject it with poison. The spines and pincers can regenerate (regrow) over and over again.

There is an opening at the top, called the anus. This is where waste materials leave the body.

The sharp spines are in rows from top to bottom.

Close up, you can see the tube feet waving around.

These special pincers can inject an attacker with poison.

BIG MOUTH

SEA SCORPIONS LURK among the seaweeds in deep tide pools, waiting to gobble up smaller fish and shrimp. These fish cannot swim fast, but they have huge mouths, so they manage to catch plenty to eat. This short-spined sea scorpion can grow up to 12 inches long. Its mottled coloring helps it hide from enemies as well as from its prey. Sea scorpions breed in winter and early spring. The females lay a mass of orange eggs, often in a crevice between the rocks. Sometimes a male digs a hollow in the bottom of the tide pool and the female lays her eggs there. The male usually guards the eggs until they hatch into tiny larvae. These swim among the plankton, and finally grow into fish in early summer.

GUESS WHAT?
Sea scorpions can turn darker or lighter to match their surroundings, and they also change color according to the seasons. Females often have bright orange bellies in the spring.

MANY NAMES
This fish is also called a bull rout, sting-fish, or father-lasher. All these names give you an idea of its fierce behavior. Sea scorpions sometimes drive away much larger fish, including sharks, from their hunting grounds. They twist their bodies quickly in the water, so that their sharp spines whip around toward the enemy and frighten it off.

Each large eye can swivel in its socket to see all around.

These short spines protect the protruding eyes.

These two holes are nostrils, called nares. The fish uses them for smelling.

Each fin is made of long bones with skin stretched between them, like the webbed foot of a duck.

Waste material leaves the body through this hole, called the anal vent.

The two pelvic fins are close together on the underside. They help support the heavy head when the fish is resting on a rock.

The mouth opens very wide, so smaller fish can be swallowed in one gulp.

The tail fin is also called the caudal fin. The fish uses it for steering.

The spiny dorsal fin on the back helps keep the fish upright.

This strong spine is formed by part of the operculum (gill cover). The spine protects the fish from attack.

Unlike most fish, this sea scorpion has smooth skin and no scales.

The pectoral fins allow the fish to balance and steer.

SPINY SCORPION
The short-spined sea scorpion does not need to swim fast to catch its food. Instead, it lies in wait for a meal to swim by. If the sea scorpion is alarmed by a larger fish, it can scare it away by raising the long, sharp spines on its operculum (gill cover). Scientists think that these spines may contain a mild poison. But they are so sharp that few predators dare to attack the fish anyway.

ROCK STARS

WHEN THE TIDE IS OUT, starfish and brittle stars hide under rocks. But when the tide comes in they leave the shelter of the rocks to search for food. Starfish are predators (hunters), and eat mussels and other shelled creatures. They pry open the shells with their strong arms, then turn their stomachs inside out over their victims to digest the animals inside. Brittle stars trap small, soft-bodied creatures between the spines on their arms, then pass the food on to the mouth. In spring and summer, starfish and brittle stars release millions of eggs into the water. The fertilized eggs develop into larvae, which float in the sea for about three weeks, then settle on the bottom of a tide pool, to grow into adults.

GUESS WHAT?
If a starfish's or brittle star's arm is broken off, a whole new animal can grow from the lost arm. Some starfish reproduce by simply pulling themselves apart to make copies of themselves.

Brittle stars only use their tube feet for passing food down to the mouth.

These rows of spines are part of the brittle star's skeleton.

The mouth is on the underside of the body.

A brittle star's arms grow all the time. If part of an arm is pulled off, the arm simply grows from the broken end.

These little spines trap all sorts of food, including small shrimp.

Few predators risk these sharp spines for such a light snack.

The brittle star wriggles its arms vigorously from side to side to move itself along.

BRITTLE ARMS

Brittle stars have special bony plates in their arms that allow them to move from side to side extremely quickly, but not up and down. A brittle star's arms are very brittle indeed, and they can break off easily. If an arm gets broken off, a new one soon grows in its place. This is called regeneration.

SPINY SKELETONS

Starfish have skeletons made of chalk inside their bodies. But parts of the skeleton also stick out of the skin, like little spines. These spines sometimes have tiny pincers on them for cleaning the arms. Starfish and brittle stars belong to the group of animals called *Echinodermata*, which means "spiny-skinned".

Starfish have suckers on their tube feet, that help them to grip on to rocks.

The starfish uses its strong tube feet for walking.

This spiny starfish has a ring of tiny pincers around each spine, used for cleaning its arms.

Starfish grasp prey with their strong arms.

The brilliant color of this scarlet serpent brittle star makes it easy to spot.

These pink tips are simple eyes. They are sensitive to light and darkness.

TRAVELING BY TUBE
Starfish and brittle stars have tube feet on the underside of their arms. Brittle stars use these to push food into their mouths. But they cannot use them for moving around, as a starfish can. Each tube foot is full of fluid. Muscles pump the fluid in and out of the feet to move them up and down. This is how a starfish walks, and how a brittle star feeds itself.

These two feathery tentacles can feel things. The sea lemon uses them to find its food.

LITTLE LEMON

THE SEA LEMON CREEPS slowly around the tide pool, searching for food. Sea lemons are sea slugs, related to whelks and other mollusks. A sea lemon moves by using the flat, muscular foot on the underside of its body. It feeds on a simple, plantlike animal called a breadcrumb sponge, which grows on rocks and under seaweed. Sea lemons have a filelike tongue, called a radula, which they use to scrape food off the rocks. They are hermaphrodites (both male and female at the same time), so any two can mate and lay eggs. These eggs hatch into larvae in the summer. They swim in the open sea for several weeks, then settle on the bottom to turn into tiny adults. They feed and grow among the rocks until spring, when they reach their full size and are ready to mate.

This sea lemon has pulled its gills back inside the body so that you cannot see them at all. This protects them from any damage.

The knobby skin and patchy coloring help disguise the sea lemon.

SNEAKY SLUG

A sea lemon has no shell to protect its soft body. Instead, it is well disguised with its mottled colors and warty skin. The sea lemon's coloring helps it blend in with the pebbles and sand, and hide from its enemies. When a sea lemon keeps absolutely still, it is very difficult to spot in the tide pool.

GUESS WHAT?

Sea lemons and other sea slugs with a ring of gills on their backs belong to a group of animals called *Nudibranchs*, which means "naked gill."

EGGY RIBBON

A sea lemon lays its eggs in a long ribbonlike coil. It glues one end on to a rock using a sticky substance called mucus, which it produces inside its body. There may be more than 500,000 eggs in one ribbon. Sea lemons have to lay such a large number because so many of their eggs and larvae are eaten by fish long before they develop into adults.

FRILLY GILLS

There is an opening called the anus on the sea lemon's back, where waste products leave the body. This opening is surrounded by a ring of lacy gills that can move in and out of the body. The sea lemon uses these gills for breathing. Some kinds of sea slugs have no gills, and they breathe through their skin instead.

There is a ring of frilly gills on the back for breathing.

The outer skin covering the upper part of the body is called the mantle.

INDEX

abdomen 16, 17
algae 20
antennae 15, 17
anus 23, 29
Aristotle's lantern 22

barbels 19
barnacles 12
beadlet anemone 9, 11
bladder wrack 9, 20, 21
brittle star 26-27
brown seaweed 20, 21

carapace 14, 16
carnivores 10, 12
chlorophyll 20, 21
claw 14, 16
color
  disguise 16, 22, 28
  sea anemone's 10
  seaweed's 20
  whelk's 12, 13
crabs 8, 9, 13, 14-15, 16-17
crustaceans 14

disguise 14, 16, 18, 22, 28
dog whelk 9, 12-13

edible crab 8, 14-15
eggs *see each animal*
enemies 14, 16, 18, 24
exoskeleton 14
eyes *see each animal*

fins 18, 19, 24, 25
fish 11, 18, 21, 22, 24, 29
five-bearded rockling 8, 18-19
foot 21, 28

giant kelp 20
gills 19, 25, 28, 29
green seaweed 20

hairs 14, 15, 16, 17, 18
hermaphrodites 28
holdfast 20

jellyfish 10

larvae *see each animal*

mollusks 12, 20, 28
mouth 10, 11, 22, 24, 26, 27
mouthparts 15, 16
mucus 21, 29
mussels 9, 12, 13, 14, 20, 26

nostrils 19, 24

operculum 13, 19, 25

photosynthesis 20, 21
piecrust crab 14-15
pincers 14, 16, 17, 23, 26, 27
plankton 17, 22, 24
poison 11, 23, 25
predators 16, 17, 22, 23, 25, 26
prey 10, 11, 24, 27
proboscis 12, 13

red seaweed 9, 20, 21
rockling 8, 18-19

scales 18, 19, 25
scarlet serpent brittle star 9, 26-27
sea anemone 9, 10-11
sea lemon 9, 28-29
sea scorpion 8, 24-25
sea slug 21, 28, 29
sea urchin 8, 22-23
seaweed 8, 9, 18, 20-21, 24
shanny 8, 18-19
shell 12, 13, 14, 16, 26
short-spined sea scorpion 8, 24-25
skeleton 22, 26
snails 12, 21
snakelocks anemone 9, 11
spines 22, 23, 24, 25, 26, 27
spiny starfish 8, 27
sponge 12, 28
starfish 8, 22, 26-27
strawberry anemone 9, 10

tentacle 10, 11, 13, 28
tide 8, 11, 19, 21, 26
tongue 12, 28
tube feet 22, 23, 26, 27

velvet swimming crab 9, 14, 16-17

whelk 9, 12-13, 28

GLOSSARY

Algae *simple plants, such as seaweeds*
Antennae *a pair of feelers*
Bivalve *a mollusk, such as a mussel, with a two-part, hinged shell*
Carapace *the top part of the exoskeleton*
Carnivorous *meat-eating*
Echinodermata *a group of sea animals with tube feet and a test*
Exoskeleton *an outer covering on the body, made from a tough substance called chitin*
Gills *organs for breathing under water*
Hermaphrodite *an animal that has both male and female parts*
Holdfast *the part of a plant, such as a seaweed, that grips on to a support*
Larva *the young, grublike stage of an animal's life*
Mantle *part of a mollusk's skin, which makes the shell*
Mollusk *a soft-bodied animal, such as a snail or slug, that often has a shell*
Nares *nostrils*

Omnivore *an animal that eats both plants and meat*
Operculum *a protective cover, such as a fish's gill cover*
Photosynthesis *the use of sunlight by plants to produce the energy to grow*
Plankton *tiny, floating sea creatures and plants*
Proboscis *the long, strawlike mouthpart of an animal, such as a whelk*
Radula *a filelike tongue*
Regeneration *the regrowth of part of the body by a plant or animal*
Scavenger *an animal that feeds on decaying plant or animal remains*
Setae *special hairs on the body*
Spores *seedlike bodies produced by many plants and simple animals when the male and female sex cells pair*
Tentacles *flexible feelers for touching, feeding, or smelling*
Test *the tough outer layer of an animal, such as a sea urchin*